VEHICLE DETAILS

Make and Model	
Registration	
Year of Registration	
Engine size/type	
VIN	
Colour	
Radio Code	
Transmission Type	
Month of MOT	
Notes	

SERVICE INSPECTION

Your service centre will advise you on the type of service your vehicle requires

Date

Mileage

Service Centre Stamp

Signature:

Service Type:

- Minor Service
- Major Service
- Inspection

Next Service Due:

Date

Or

Mileage

Work Carried Out:

- Engine/Oil Filter
- Air Filter
- Fuel Filter
- Dust Filter
- Coolant
- Brake Fluid
- Transmission Fluid
- Timing/Cam Belt
- Spark Plugs
- Brake Pads
- Brake Discs
- Battery

Notes:

Date

Mileage

Service Centre Stamp

Signature:

Service Type:

- Minor Service
- Major Service
- Inspection

Next Service Due:

Date

Or

Mileage

Work Carried Out:

- Engine/Oil Filter
- Air Filter
- Fuel Filter
- Dust Filter
- Coolant
- Brake Fluid
- Transmission Fluid
- Timing/Cam Belt
- Spark Plugs
- Brake Pads
- Brake Discs
- Battery

Notes:

SERVICE INSPECTION

Your service centre will advise you on the type of service your vehicle requires

Date

Mileage

Service Centre Stamp

Signature:

Service Type:

- Minor Service
- Major Service
- Inspection

Next Service Due:

Date

Or

Mileage

Work Carried Out:

- Engine/Oil Filter
- Air Filter
- Fuel Filter
- Dust Filter
- Coolant
- Brake Fluid
- Transmission Fluid
- Timing/Cam Belt
- Spark Plugs
- Brake Pads
- Brake Discs
- Battery

Notes:

Date

Mileage

Service Centre Stamp

Signature:

Service Type:

- Minor Service
- Major Service
- Inspection

Next Service Due:

Date

Or

Mileage

Work Carried Out:

- Engine/Oil Filter
- Air Filter
- Fuel Filter
- Dust Filter
- Coolant
- Brake Fluid
- Transmission Fluid
- Timing/Cam Belt
- Spark Plugs
- Brake Pads
- Brake Discs
- Battery

Notes:

SERVICE INSPECTION

Your service centre will advise you on the type of service your vehicle requires

Date

Mileage

Service Centre Stamp

Signature:

Service Type:

- Minor Service
- Major Service
- Inspection

Next Service Due:

Date

Or

Mileage

Work Carried Out:

- Engine/Oil Filter
- Air Filter
- Fuel Filter
- Dust Filter
- Coolant
- Brake Fluid
- Transmission Fluid
- Timing/Cam Belt
- Spark Plugs
- Brake Pads
- Brake Discs
- Battery

Notes:

Date

Mileage

Service Centre Stamp

Signature:

Service Type:

- Minor Service
- Major Service
- Inspection

Next Service Due:

Date

Or

Mileage

Work Carried Out:

- Engine/Oil Filter
- Air Filter
- Fuel Filter
- Dust Filter
- Coolant
- Brake Fluid
- Transmission Fluid
- Timing/Cam Belt
- Spark Plugs
- Brake Pads
- Brake Discs
- Battery

Notes:

SERVICE INSPECTION

Your service centre will advise you on the type of service your vehicle requires

Date

Mileage

Service Centre Stamp

Signature:

Service Type:

- Minor Service
- Major Service
- Inspection

Next Service Due:

Date

Or

Mileage

Work Carried Out:

- Engine/Oil Filter
- Air Filter
- Fuel Filter
- Dust Filter
- Coolant
- Brake Fluid
- Transmission Fluid
- Timing/Cam Belt
- Spark Plugs
- Brake Pads
- Brake Discs
- Battery

Notes:

Date

Mileage

Service Centre Stamp

Signature:

Service Type:

- Minor Service
- Major Service
- Inspection

Next Service Due:

Date

Or

Mileage

Work Carried Out:

- Engine/Oil Filter
- Air Filter
- Fuel Filter
- Dust Filter
- Coolant
- Brake Fluid
- Transmission Fluid
- Timing/Cam Belt
- Spark Plugs
- Brake Pads
- Brake Discs
- Battery

Notes:

SERVICE INSPECTION

Your service centre will advise you on the type of service your vehicle requires

Date

Mileage

Service Centre Stamp

Signature:

Service Type:

- Minor Service
- Major Service
- Inspection

Next Service Due:

Date

Or

Mileage

Work Carried Out:

- Engine/Oil Filter
- Air Filter
- Fuel Filter
- Dust Filter
- Coolant
- Brake Fluid
- Transmission Fluid
- Timing/Cam Belt
- Spark Plugs
- Brake Pads
- Brake Discs
- Battery

Notes:

Date

Mileage

Service Centre Stamp

Signature:

Service Type:

- Minor Service
- Major Service
- Inspection

Next Service Due:

Date

Or

Mileage

Work Carried Out:

- Engine/Oil Filter
- Air Filter
- Fuel Filter
- Dust Filter
- Coolant
- Brake Fluid
- Transmission Fluid
- Timing/Cam Belt
- Spark Plugs
- Brake Pads
- Brake Discs
- Battery

Notes:

SERVICE INSPECTION

Your service centre will advise you on the type of service your vehicle requires

Date | Mileage

Service Centre Stamp

Signature:

Service Type:
- Minor Service
- Major Service
- Inspection

Next Service Due:

Date

Or

Mileage

Work Carried Out:
- Engine/Oil Filter
- Air Filter
- Fuel Filter
- Dust Filter
- Coolant
- Brake Fluid
- Transmission Fluid
- Timing/Cam Belt
- Spark Plugs
- Brake Pads
- Brake Discs
- Battery

Notes:

Date | Mileage

Service Centre Stamp

Signature:

Service Type:
- Minor Service
- Major Service
- Inspection

Next Service Due:

Date

Or

Mileage

Work Carried Out:
- Engine/Oil Filter
- Air Filter
- Fuel Filter
- Dust Filter
- Coolant
- Brake Fluid
- Transmission Fluid
- Timing/Cam Belt
- Spark Plugs
- Brake Pads
- Brake Discs
- Battery

Notes:

SERVICE INSPECTION

Your service centre will advise you on the type of service your vehicle requires

Date

Mileage

Service Centre Stamp

Signature:

Service Type:

- Minor Service
- Major Service
- Inspection

Next Service Due:

Date

Or

Mileage

Work Carried Out:

- Engine/Oil Filter
- Air Filter
- Fuel Filter
- Dust Filter
- Coolant
- Brake Fluid
- Transmission Fluid
- Timing/Cam Belt
- Spark Plugs
- Brake Pads
- Brake Discs
- Battery

Notes:

Date

Mileage

Service Centre Stamp

Signature:

Service Type:

- Minor Service
- Major Service
- Inspection

Next Service Due:

Date

Or

Mileage

Work Carried Out:

- Engine/Oil Filter
- Air Filter
- Fuel Filter
- Dust Filter
- Coolant
- Brake Fluid
- Transmission Fluid
- Timing/Cam Belt
- Spark Plugs
- Brake Pads
- Brake Discs
- Battery

Notes:

SERVICE INSPECTION

Your service centre will advise you on the type of service your vehicle requires

Date

Mileage

Service Centre Stamp

Signature:

Service Type:

- Minor Service
- Major Service
- Inspection

Next Service Due:

Date

Or

Mileage

Work Carried Out:

- Engine/Oil Filter
- Air Filter
- Fuel Filter
- Dust Filter
- Coolant
- Brake Fluid
- Transmission Fluid
- Timing/Cam Belt
- Spark Plugs
- Brake Pads
- Brake Discs
- Battery

Notes:

Date

Mileage

Service Centre Stamp

Signature:

Service Type:

- Minor Service
- Major Service
- Inspection

Next Service Due:

Date

Or

Mileage

Work Carried Out:

- Engine/Oil Filter
- Air Filter
- Fuel Filter
- Dust Filter
- Coolant
- Brake Fluid
- Transmission Fluid
- Timing/Cam Belt
- Spark Plugs
- Brake Pads
- Brake Discs
- Battery

Notes:

SERVICE INSPECTION

Your service centre will advise you on the type of service your vehicle requires

Date | Mileage

Service Centre Stamp

Signature:

Service Type:

- Minor Service
- Major Service
- Inspection

Next Service Due:

Date

Or

Mileage

Work Carried Out:

- Engine/Oil Filter
- Air Filter
- Fuel Filter
- Dust Filter
- Coolant
- Brake Fluid
- Transmission Fluid
- Timing/Cam Belt
- Spark Plugs
- Brake Pads
- Brake Discs
- Battery

Notes:

Date | Mileage

Service Centre Stamp

Signature:

Service Type:

- Minor Service
- Major Service
- Inspection

Next Service Due:

Date

Or

Mileage

Work Carried Out:

- Engine/Oil Filter
- Air Filter
- Fuel Filter
- Dust Filter
- Coolant
- Brake Fluid
- Transmission Fluid
- Timing/Cam Belt
- Spark Plugs
- Brake Pads
- Brake Discs
- Battery

Notes:

SERVICE INSPECTION

Your service centre will advise you on the type of service your vehicle requires

Date

Mileage

Service Centre Stamp

Signature:

Service Type:

- Minor Service
- Major Service
- Inspection

Next Service Due:

Date

Or

Mileage

Work Carried Out:

- Engine/Oil Filter
- Air Filter
- Fuel Filter
- Dust Filter
- Coolant
- Brake Fluid
- Transmission Fluid
- Timing/Cam Belt
- Spark Plugs
- Brake Pads
- Brake Discs
- Battery

Notes:

Date

Mileage

Service Centre Stamp

Signature:

Service Type:

- Minor Service
- Major Service
- Inspection

Next Service Due:

Date

Or

Mileage

Work Carried Out:

- Engine/Oil Filter
- Air Filter
- Fuel Filter
- Dust Filter
- Coolant
- Brake Fluid
- Transmission Fluid
- Timing/Cam Belt
- Spark Plugs
- Brake Pads
- Brake Discs
- Battery

Notes:

SERVICE INSPECTION

Your service centre will advise you on the type of service your vehicle requires

Date

Mileage

Service Centre Stamp

Signature:

Service Type:

- Minor Service
- Major Service
- Inspection

Next Service Due:

Date

Or

Mileage

Work Carried Out:

- Engine/Oil Filter
- Air Filter
- Fuel Filter
- Dust Filter
- Coolant
- Brake Fluid
- Transmission Fluid
- Timing/Cam Belt
- Spark Plugs
- Brake Pads
- Brake Discs
- Battery

Notes:

Date

Mileage

Service Centre Stamp

Signature:

Service Type:

- Minor Service
- Major Service
- Inspection

Next Service Due:

Date

Or

Mileage

Work Carried Out:

- Engine/Oil Filter
- Air Filter
- Fuel Filter
- Dust Filter
- Coolant
- Brake Fluid
- Transmission Fluid
- Timing/Cam Belt
- Spark Plugs
- Brake Pads
- Brake Discs
- Battery

Notes:

SERVICE INSPECTION

Your service centre will advise you on the type of service your vehicle requires

Date

Mileage

Service Centre Stamp

Signature:

Service Type:

- Minor Service
- Major Service
- Inspection

Next Service Due:

Date

Or

Mileage

Work Carried Out:

- Engine/Oil Filter
- Air Filter
- Fuel Filter
- Dust Filter
- Coolant
- Brake Fluid
- Transmission Fluid
- Timing/Cam Belt
- Spark Plugs
- Brake Pads
- Brake Discs
- Battery

Notes:

Date

Mileage

Service Centre Stamp

Signature:

Service Type:

- Minor Service
- Major Service
- Inspection

Next Service Due:

Date

Or

Mileage

Work Carried Out:

- Engine/Oil Filter
- Air Filter
- Fuel Filter
- Dust Filter
- Coolant
- Brake Fluid
- Transmission Fluid
- Timing/Cam Belt
- Spark Plugs
- Brake Pads
- Brake Discs
- Battery

Notes:

SERVICE INSPECTION

Your service centre will advise you on the type of service your vehicle requires

Date

Mileage

Service Centre Stamp

Signature:

Service Type:

- Minor Service
- Major Service
- Inspection

Next Service Due:

Date

Or

Mileage

Work Carried Out:

- Engine/Oil Filter
- Air Filter
- Fuel Filter
- Dust Filter
- Coolant
- Brake Fluid
- Transmission Fluid
- Timing/Cam Belt
- Spark Plugs
- Brake Pads
- Brake Discs
- Battery

Notes:

Date

Mileage

Service Centre Stamp

Signature:

Service Type:

- Minor Service
- Major Service
- Inspection

Next Service Due:

Date

Or

Mileage

Work Carried Out:

- Engine/Oil Filter
- Air Filter
- Fuel Filter
- Dust Filter
- Coolant
- Brake Fluid
- Transmission Fluid
- Timing/Cam Belt
- Spark Plugs
- Brake Pads
- Brake Discs
- Battery

Notes:

SERVICE INSPECTION

Your service centre will advise you on the type of service your vehicle requires

Date | Mileage

Service Centre Stamp

Signature:

Service Type:
- Minor Service
- Major Service
- Inspection

Next Service Due:
Date
Or
Mileage

Work Carried Out:
- Engine/Oil Filter
- Air Filter
- Fuel Filter
- Dust Filter
- Coolant
- Brake Fluid
- Transmission Fluid
- Timing/Cam Belt
- Spark Plugs
- Brake Pads
- Brake Discs
- Battery

Notes:

Date | Mileage

Service Centre Stamp

Signature:

Service Type:
- Minor Service
- Major Service
- Inspection

Next Service Due:
Date
Or
Mileage

Work Carried Out:
- Engine/Oil Filter
- Air Filter
- Fuel Filter
- Dust Filter
- Coolant
- Brake Fluid
- Transmission Fluid
- Timing/Cam Belt
- Spark Plugs
- Brake Pads
- Brake Discs
- Battery

Notes:

SERVICE INSPECTION

Your service centre will advise you on the type of service your vehicle requires

Date

Mileage

Service Centre Stamp

Signature:

Service Type:

- Minor Service
- Major Service
- Inspection

Next Service Due:

Date

Or

Mileage

Work Carried Out:

- Engine/Oil Filter
- Air Filter
- Fuel Filter
- Dust Filter
- Coolant
- Brake Fluid
- Transmission Fluid
- Timing/Cam Belt
- Spark Plugs
- Brake Pads
- Brake Discs
- Battery

Notes:

Date

Mileage

Service Centre Stamp

Signature:

Service Type:

- Minor Service
- Major Service
- Inspection

Next Service Due:

Date

Or

Mileage

Work Carried Out:

- Engine/Oil Filter
- Air Filter
- Fuel Filter
- Dust Filter
- Coolant
- Brake Fluid
- Transmission Fluid
- Timing/Cam Belt
- Spark Plugs
- Brake Pads
- Brake Discs
- Battery

Notes:

SERVICE INSPECTION

Your service centre will advise you on the type of service your vehicle requires

Date

Mileage

Service Centre Stamp

Signature:

Service Type:

- [ ] Minor Service
- [ ] Major Service
- [ ] Inspection

Next Service Due:

Date

Or

Mileage

Work Carried Out:

- [ ] Engine/Oil Filter
- [ ] Air Filter
- [ ] Fuel Filter
- [ ] Dust Filter
- [ ] Coolant
- [ ] Brake Fluid
- [ ] Transmission Fluid
- [ ] Timing/Cam Belt
- [ ] Spark Plugs
- [ ] Brake Pads
- [ ] Brake Discs
- [ ] Battery

Notes:

Date

Mileage

Service Centre Stamp

Signature:

Service Type:

- [ ] Minor Service
- [ ] Major Service
- [ ] Inspection

Next Service Due:

Date

Or

Mileage

Work Carried Out:

- [ ] Engine/Oil Filter
- [ ] Air Filter
- [ ] Fuel Filter
- [ ] Dust Filter
- [ ] Coolant
- [ ] Brake Fluid
- [ ] Transmission Fluid
- [ ] Timing/Cam Belt
- [ ] Spark Plugs
- [ ] Brake Pads
- [ ] Brake Discs
- [ ] Battery

Notes:

SERVICE INSPECTION

Your service centre will advise you on the type of service your vehicle requires

Date

Mileage

Service Centre Stamp

Signature:

Service Type:

- Minor Service
- Major Service
- Inspection

Next Service Due:

Date

Or

Mileage

Work Carried Out:

- Engine/Oil Filter
- Air Filter
- Fuel Filter
- Dust Filter
- Coolant
- Brake Fluid
- Transmission Fluid
- Timing/Cam Belt
- Spark Plugs
- Brake Pads
- Brake Discs
- Battery

Notes:

Date

Mileage

Service Centre Stamp

Signature:

Service Type:

- Minor Service
- Major Service
- Inspection

Next Service Due:

Date

Or

Mileage

Work Carried Out:

- Engine/Oil Filter
- Air Filter
- Fuel Filter
- Dust Filter
- Coolant
- Brake Fluid
- Transmission Fluid
- Timing/Cam Belt
- Spark Plugs
- Brake Pads
- Brake Discs
- Battery

Notes:

SERVICE INSPECTION

Your service centre will advise you on the type of service your vehicle requires

Date

Mileage

Service Centre Stamp

Signature:

Service Type:

- Minor Service
- Major Service
- Inspection

Next Service Due:

Date

Or

Mileage

Work Carried Out:

- Engine/Oil Filter
- Air Filter
- Fuel Filter
- Dust Filter
- Coolant
- Brake Fluid
- Transmission Fluid
- Timing/Cam Belt
- Spark Plugs
- Brake Pads
- Brake Discs
- Battery

Notes:

Date

Mileage

Service Centre Stamp

Signature:

Service Type:

- Minor Service
- Major Service
- Inspection

Next Service Due:

Date

Or

Mileage

Work Carried Out:

- Engine/Oil Filter
- Air Filter
- Fuel Filter
- Dust Filter
- Coolant
- Brake Fluid
- Transmission Fluid
- Timing/Cam Belt
- Spark Plugs
- Brake Pads
- Brake Discs
- Battery

Notes:

SERVICE INSPECTION

Your service centre will advise you on the type of service your vehicle requires

Date

Mileage

Service Centre Stamp

Signature:

Service Type:

- Minor Service
- Major Service
- Inspection

Next Service Due:

Date

Or

Mileage

Work Carried Out:

- Engine/Oil Filter
- Air Filter
- Fuel Filter
- Dust Filter
- Coolant
- Brake Fluid
- Transmission Fluid
- Timing/Cam Belt
- Spark Plugs
- Brake Pads
- Brake Discs
- Battery

Notes:

Date

Mileage

Service Centre Stamp

Signature:

Service Type:

- Minor Service
- Major Service
- Inspection

Next Service Due:

Date

Or

Mileage

Work Carried Out:

- Engine/Oil Filter
- Air Filter
- Fuel Filter
- Dust Filter
- Coolant
- Brake Fluid
- Transmission Fluid
- Timing/Cam Belt
- Spark Plugs
- Brake Pads
- Brake Discs
- Battery

Notes:

SERVICE INSPECTION

Your service centre will advise you on the type of service your vehicle requires

Date

Mileage

Service Centre Stamp

Signature:

Service Type:

- Minor Service
- Major Service
- Inspection

Next Service Due:

Date

Or

Mileage

Work Carried Out:

- Engine/Oil Filter
- Air Filter
- Fuel Filter
- Dust Filter
- Coolant
- Brake Fluid
- Transmission Fluid
- Timing/Cam Belt
- Spark Plugs
- Brake Pads
- Brake Discs
- Battery

Notes:

Date

Mileage

Service Centre Stamp

Signature:

Service Type:

- Minor Service
- Major Service
- Inspection

Next Service Due:

Date

Or

Mileage

Work Carried Out:

- Engine/Oil Filter
- Air Filter
- Fuel Filter
- Dust Filter
- Coolant
- Brake Fluid
- Transmission Fluid
- Timing/Cam Belt
- Spark Plugs
- Brake Pads
- Brake Discs
- Battery

Notes:

SERVICE INSPECTION

Your service centre will advise you on the type of service your vehicle requires

Date | Mileage

Service Centre Stamp

Signature:

Service Type:
- Minor Service
- Major Service
- Inspection

Next Service Due:
- Date
- Or
- Mileage

Work Carried Out:
- Engine/Oil Filter
- Air Filter
- Fuel Filter
- Dust Filter
- Coolant
- Brake Fluid
- Transmission Fluid
- Timing/Cam Belt
- Spark Plugs
- Brake Pads
- Brake Discs
- Battery

Notes:

Date | Mileage

Service Centre Stamp

Signature:

Service Type:
- Minor Service
- Major Service
- Inspection

Next Service Due:
- Date
- Or
- Mileage

Work Carried Out:
- Engine/Oil Filter
- Air Filter
- Fuel Filter
- Dust Filter
- Coolant
- Brake Fluid
- Transmission Fluid
- Timing/Cam Belt
- Spark Plugs
- Brake Pads
- Brake Discs
- Battery

Notes:

SERVICE INSPECTION

Your service centre will advise you on the type of service your vehicle requires

Date

Mileage

Service Centre Stamp

Signature:

Service Type:

- Minor Service
- Major Service
- Inspection

Next Service Due:

Date

Or

Mileage

Work Carried Out:

- Engine/Oil Filter
- Air Filter
- Fuel Filter
- Dust Filter
- Coolant
- Brake Fluid
- Transmission Fluid
- Timing/Cam Belt
- Spark Plugs
- Brake Pads
- Brake Discs
- Battery

Notes:

Date

Mileage

Service Centre Stamp

Signature:

Service Type:

- Minor Service
- Major Service
- Inspection

Next Service Due:

Date

Or

Mileage

Work Carried Out:

- Engine/Oil Filter
- Air Filter
- Fuel Filter
- Dust Filter
- Coolant
- Brake Fluid
- Transmission Fluid
- Timing/Cam Belt
- Spark Plugs
- Brake Pads
- Brake Discs
- Battery

Notes:

SERVICE INSPECTION

Your service centre will advise you on the type of service your vehicle requires

Date
Mileage
Service Centre Stamp
Signature:

Service Type:
- Minor Service
- Major Service
- Inspection

Next Service Due:
Date
Or
Mileage

Work Carried Out:
- Engine/Oil Filter
- Air Filter
- Fuel Filter
- Dust Filter
- Coolant
- Brake Fluid
- Transmission Fluid
- Timing/Cam Belt
- Spark Plugs
- Brake Pads
- Brake Discs
- Battery

Notes:

Date
Mileage
Service Centre Stamp
Signature:

Service Type:
- Minor Service
- Major Service
- Inspection

Next Service Due:
Date
Or
Mileage

Work Carried Out:
- Engine/Oil Filter
- Air Filter
- Fuel Filter
- Dust Filter
- Coolant
- Brake Fluid
- Transmission Fluid
- Timing/Cam Belt
- Spark Plugs
- Brake Pads
- Brake Discs
- Battery

Notes:

SERVICE INSPECTION

Your service centre will advise you on the type of service your vehicle requires

Date

Mileage

Service Centre Stamp

Signature:

Service Type:

- Minor Service
- Major Service
- Inspection

Next Service Due:

Date

Or

Mileage

Work Carried Out:

- Engine/Oil Filter
- Air Filter
- Fuel Filter
- Dust Filter
- Coolant
- Brake Fluid
- Transmission Fluid
- Timing/Cam Belt
- Spark Plugs
- Brake Pads
- Brake Discs
- Battery

Notes:

Date

Mileage

Service Centre Stamp

Signature:

Service Type:

- Minor Service
- Major Service
- Inspection

Next Service Due:

Date

Or

Mileage

Work Carried Out:

- Engine/Oil Filter
- Air Filter
- Fuel Filter
- Dust Filter
- Coolant
- Brake Fluid
- Transmission Fluid
- Timing/Cam Belt
- Spark Plugs
- Brake Pads
- Brake Discs
- Battery

Notes:

SERVICE INSPECTION

Your service centre will advise you on the type of service your vehicle requires

Date

Mileage

Service Centre Stamp

Signature:

Service Type:

- Minor Service
- Major Service
- Inspection

Next Service Due:

Date

Or

Mileage

Work Carried Out:

- Engine/Oil Filter
- Air Filter
- Fuel Filter
- Dust Filter
- Coolant
- Brake Fluid
- Transmission Fluid
- Timing/Cam Belt
- Spark Plugs
- Brake Pads
- Brake Discs
- Battery

Notes:

Date

Mileage

Service Centre Stamp

Signature:

Service Type:

- Minor Service
- Major Service
- Inspection

Next Service Due:

Date

Or

Mileage

Work Carried Out:

- Engine/Oil Filter
- Air Filter
- Fuel Filter
- Dust Filter
- Coolant
- Brake Fluid
- Transmission Fluid
- Timing/Cam Belt
- Spark Plugs
- Brake Pads
- Brake Discs
- Battery

Notes:

Printed in Great Britain
by Amazon

21739918R00020